OF THE
SIREN

SONG OF THE SIREN

Tales of Rhythm and Revolution

DANA BRYANT

Boulevard Books, New York

"Canis Rufus," which was called "Can't Be Music," appeared in *Bomb* magazine in Winter 1993, issue 42, and in *Straight No Chaser*, Spring/Summer 1992.

"At a Quarter to Five" appeared in *Bomb* magazine, Winter 1993.

"Housecleaning" and "Fantasy Lover #5" both appeared in *Aloud: Voices from the Nuyorican Poets Cafe* from Henry Holt, 1994.

SONG OF THE SIREN: TALES OF RHYTHM AND REVOLUTION

A Boulevard Book / published by arrangement with the author

PRINTING HISTORY
Boulevard trade paperback edition / October 1995

ISBN: 1-57297-004-9

BOULEVARD
Boulevard Books are published by The Berkley Publishing
Group, 200 Madison Avenue, New York, New York 10016.
BOULEVARD and its logo are trademarks belonging to
Berkley Publishing Corporation.

PRINTED IN THE UNITED STATES OF AMERICA

10 9 8 7 6 5 4 3 2 1

To Baby Ruth, Teddy,
Doris, and May-May

CONTENTS

MEANING SONG
The Poetry of Dana Bryant

She is our Sappho.

Dana Bryant's poetry is music where the head tilts back and wails, where the language that emerges surges like a flash flood into every available space. You didn't know there were so many unlit corridors until her voice started turning on the lights. And, yes, I am talking about the flickering candlelight of memory, the outlines of love. And, yes, the fractured mirrorball of disco frenzy pumping raw. And, yes, the blinding spotlight revealing. . . .

Dana Bryant herself, striding into the Nuyorican Poets Cafe, spring 1991, and finding a room dedicated to poetry, where Word Rules. This is Dana Bryant, "sort of" a singer/songwriter, who finds at the Cafe ease and inspiration in the company of poets. She begins to let the words speak for themselves, a cappella, discovering a music inside language. At Steve Cannon's Stoop she locates the exact spot where speech breaks into melody, where meaning percusses. This is what it means to discover you are a poet.

And from this simple revelation an entire era crumbles. No longer would the dynamic be a one way: poet turns rocker/poet works with music backup/to get word out/just to be heard/to find an audience that poetry, as heretofore defined, had left outside someplace. Here was a musician deciding she no longer needed those trappings, that she could return to the root, the poetry of the thing.

And, specifically, a poetry rooted in her past. In the African-American culture of the deep South: the family, the food, the Church, the land itself. A poetry that migrates from Cheraw, South Carolina, up North, to Brooklyn, Bed-Stuy, Flatbush. A poetry that grows up, girl to woman, full of tough wonder. A poetry that takes on the cadences and metaphors of all manner of Black dialects, that shreds stereotypes and honors a new arcana comprised of real heroes like Chaka Khan and Ntozake Shange and bell hooks. A poetry that is astonishingly, vividly unafraid to unfurl the completeness of a Woman, her passions, her fashions, her sensations, her fears and loves and sick-to-deathness of it all. Characters bolt out of the words, grow up, bop, shoot pool, go to Church, fan themselves with funeral fans, die. Violence, gentleness, pride. Life's parade in a song that sings itself.

If you are coming to this book from Dana's performances with the Nuyorican Poets Cafe Live! you will find all her greatest hits—I mean poems—included. And, of course, now that she has blazed trails for new poetry, she can move with ease back to fronting the band, be it the Groove Collective or Ronnie Jordan's, and if you are coming to this book from her music dates or her recordings—hey, this book is the key to the secrets of the inner workings, the Word word. And if this book is your introduction to Dana Bryant, let these texts lead you to sound, slide the meanings over your tongue, give full reign to the juiciness and sensuous complexities of these poems as you create a voice that lives.

> The voice which
> Is this book which
> Is the celebration
> That is Dana Bryant.

Bob Holman,
NYC, 11/94

HEAT

EXTREME
heat
was never a discomfort
rather it
brought back
memories
of time she spent
in the south

watching the
older
greyhaired woman
in a multicolored
floral dress
fanning herself

discreetly

                    in the waiting room at penn station

reminded her

                  she was
                  pulled into the gesture

the way one may
sometimes be
drawn into a yawn
she was
brought back

to that time
nigh twenty years past
the

                      pee   dee
                      baptist   church
              in cheraw south carolina

where elderly women
could be heard to sing a
righteous gospel
very well

whilst
fanning themselves
continuously

                        between
                        the hallelujahs and the amens

their   (
round brown
arms and bellies
swathed
in too tight dresses
pomaded
tightly curled hair
peeking out from under
rakishly positioned
straw
hats

and she remembers

                        the fans

prefabricated numbers
distributed by
the mamie parson's
home
of
everlasting
peace

complete
with a photograph of
bo paunch mccall's
youngest daughter
amelia

plastered
to the flip side

her honey brown face
was directed heavenward
a surprisingly
knowing smile
on her
pious lips.
smooth
caramel hands
clasped in supplication and obedience

i want to give you devotion

and she remembers
sittin' next to
mrs. thunderbird
in the third pew
how enormous
she appeared to a girl of three
buttressed up by an ample bottom
supported by slender calves
she seemed
regally
enthroned

pellets of
sweat
glistened
on the bridge of her nose
n above her upper lip
they coalesced
into tiny rivulets
which
      trickled
           down her chin
               through plateaus
                   and creases

                              permanently etched
                    in her neck

              to disappear
in the secret place
              between

                    her breasts

                                        thank
                                          youje-sus!

though sweat
pooled
in the ample armpits
of jett thunderbird
and soaked her dress
into the crack of her ass
she never acknowledged any discomfort
but regally rocked
back and forth
in
it
          hallelujah. . . .
                    amen. . . .

yes
twenty years later
when other folks
curse n swear
at the heat
and look to her
for agreement
she can only stare on
with complete incomprehension
she can
tolerate
extre-e-me
heat
welcome it even
surrender herself to it

coyly
and only
seem
to sweat
where

       her breasts
          try
     to meet. . . .

DOMINICAN GIRDLES

I was never one of those
big legged mamas
brothers was always
wet dreamin' about
and I could
            never
                        understand
why

Every other woman
in my family was
adequately equipped
and fortified
wid
brickhouse figures
of the most
                        monstrous
                        proportions

At thirteen
the most I could hope for
was the
occasional
absentminded
comment
about the
size
shape
and exact location
of my
                        hard nippled / bra-less breasts / 'neath that /
                        $14.99/Marcy's special/purple polyester/ribbed knit
                        HALTER TOP
which I wore
FIVE

out of every seven days that summer

But what I
really coveted
were those
extra special/sashayin'/double-seaters
my cousin
                    Big Gal
          sported   shamelessly

$$\begin{bmatrix} \text{thirty four} \\ \text{twenty four} \\ \text{FORTY FOUR} \end{bmatrix}$$

I'm talkin' depth and width

Weeks passed . . .
and I wuz still waitin'
for the blessed event
of puberty to
inflate particular
body parts

I wanted to know

what it meant to be
trussed up like a turkey
to hear heated sighs from my
balcony window
to be taken
eager
wet
like Zake sometimes got
OH YES

Askia Phillips
dope party

was in three days and I was invited

Well
not exactly invited . . .

me n about 5 other
girls wuz
sittin' on my stoop
satelliting Sepia
(basking in the glow
of her new girl on the block
popularity)
                    when Baybra Jones
half-stepped
and
shimmied
up the block
straight up in her face

                    Yo
                    Whatsup
                    Mama Sparkle and Shine
                    Right on Be Free Baby Love
                    Goddamn

I was undone
here
in living color
was the effigy
to whom I had
lit the candles of my
unrequited love
nightly

but I went to Brooklyn Tech
He was strictly Erasmus Hall

I watched
breathlessly
as he slid his
three by five
graffitied party invitation
into her left palm

Sepia
Goddess
was, by some strange twist of fate
to return home on Wednesday
two days before the party
it was my stoop so I
naturally
was invited to
serve as proxy
to serve/as sacrificial lamb/led to social slaughter/with
no ass
no hips
I was devastated

Until
my bestfriend
Rosa
hipped me to a sure thing
the one means
by which I could
improve my
deficit
assets . . .

Dominican Girdles

Pocket Padders   Bootie Boosters

The ones we'd seen pictures of
in the back of Essence Magazine
Which I could not afford

BUT

Two hours before that party
My
Narrow Waist
Cinched
by my mother's
Big Black Belt
My
Oiled
Soft and Sheen
Finely Picked
Neatly Patted
Sister Angela
Afro
Standing at
FULL
attention

My
Spindly Legs
teetering on
too small buffalo sandals

My
Tiny Drawers
Packed
with
every
scrap of fabric
I could find
from my mother's
sewing basket

I stood

before myself in
Rosa's mirror
swaying

my makeshift hips
in ways she'd instructed

a sight

before tonight
unseen in the
streets of Flatbush

a sight

who'd only recently
discovered the meaning
of the term
Feminine Wiles

THE PROMISED LAND

In
sixty-eight
my Presbyterian-bred mother
finally bought beanpies
from the righteous
cloth-capped brother
at the corner store
(crescent moon cradlin' the north star)
who kept callin "BLACK"
alla dat
she
had
known
to be cull-ed
or knee-grow
or
(in testier tones)
"*our* people"
"no-count-good-for-nothins"
though
                              never
"Nigras"
                                    yes

looklike
your
stealin' away to Jesus
made a change in her
somethin'
quite

large
and
sweet

with meaning

as the T.V. screen
crackled
   silver

              white

                   grey

                        senselessness
                              moans
                        violet
                   screams
         transitions
she wept
more silent than the rest
but she did indeed
weep

SECOND COUSIN

M-A-A-Hgrit?
MAHgret?
Mahgrit IMa TE-E-LL!
M-A-A-H-grit!

Lil' Bit
your sista
stumblin down the road behin us
dirt settlin on her
shoeless feet
sepia dirt
dry 'n hot
the air so open
her sour screams are
caught up
swallowed
n spit out
as tiny pinpricks of sound

C'AIN'T STANHA AWWAYS FOLLOWIN BAHIND ME!

it was why i loved you
we wuz runnin away
didn't know there'd be so much
timedust
stirred up
behind that day . . .

MAHGRET.

M..A..R..
G..A..R..
E..T..
you taught me how to spell your name
n I've never forgotten its spell

not even in winter
when i wuz alone
n contemplatin
the back yard tree
from outta my bedroom window
that
only tree
stripped bare of shade
by autumn wind
and thin from too much summer
i thought it dropped dead each season
cause it had just about enough
of protectin' us from the
hot sun
too many months of
pitty pat n spades
played on my mother's
deck chairs
you always won . . .

MAHGRET.

that first sign of blood
revealed
you proud 'n arrogant
droppin' your drawers
gingerly
showin me that
contraption
the thin elastic belt
hammocking
a wide cotton strip
one small red dot
at its center
cubicle skin
fleetingly shown
in the vestibule

before
my mother arrived
to usher us in
for
peanut butter n jelly
sandwiches
with
individually cartoned
public school milk

sunny and dale
smiled back at us
that day
and they knew why. . . .

MAHGRET.

your taut chest skin
suddenly evidenced
imperfections
each tiny mound
a week before
seamless and flat
was now
perfectly swollen
tender to the touch
brown rubber bubbles
in our bathwater

i thought it was cancer

was careful to tell you
and in our solemnity
we broke the news to
mommie. . . .

MAHGRET.

First: blood
Second: cousins

n you always got the better of it
cause you never took no mess
JUST like yaDaddy
n couldn't nobody
talk about yaMama
cause your mother?
wuz
SIX FEET UNDER, Chee!
N ANY*body gonna talk*
about huh, gotta
talk wid ME!!
Y-E-E-E-AH BUDdy!
you wuz
HARD
SPITfighter
the SIXTHborn
with the
SHARPest
TONGUE! . . .

when i heard about
that last fight
the one you
didn't win
i wouldn't believe 'em
cause we was
twelve together
not me
thirteen
the next year
and you
nothing
that same next
and i waited

after the wreaths
and camellias
were gathered
together on the back porch
after the
black dresses
had been re-pressed
and put away til
next time
i waited

i

waited . . .

COLOR BLOCKING

she had been led to believe

a quick tumble in the hay
could never really constitute
a breach of family ethics
or esthetics
so when her father
slipped
and called the boy
she had been dating
for the past five months
a cracker?
she mistakenly believed
he was likening
the golden cracked wheat
color
of her lover's skin
to a particular brand
of tea biscuit
which had always been her favorite

could a more apt description
be given of a man
who purposefully left
two dozen blue roses
on her doorstep
every monday morning

just because she'd
read him
her first poem
blue monday?

she'd been given to understand

a mind is a
terrible thing to waste
so when all her best senses
screamed in unison
that she should indeed
take and drink
the richly deserved
and sorely needed
offering of love
from his cupped hands

        she did
               without hesitation

she had been raised to dispel
from her reality
all traces of the american myth
of inequality
she developed a rock solid
belief that hers
was a right
to pick and choose
the best
fruits
from the
trees
of life
and couldn't understand why her father
choked on the bones of his own
reservations simply
because this time
she'd chosen a bose pear

she knew the blackest berries
held the sweetest juice because
she loved herself
she just loved him too

all signs indicated
she'd grown free to choose
in the same way
a flower
turns to the sun for nourishment
or
a cat
may sometimes
without provocation
be seen to bask
in a moonlight
she'd turned toward a man
bright enuf
to share her best quality
a certain skill
for transcending
the fear
of color blocking

RELIGION

i am purest when seen through your eyes
thoughtful
clear
never suspect
always colorful
and
real juicy
like a tart plum
bitten straight through to its heart
its purple skin
ripped apart and ingested
its juices
staining your teeth
as you tasted the meat of me
and found me good
and told me so
after
                              i trusted your judgment
because your mama said
you wuz born in a tiny woodshed
on a tiny island
and on that day
rivers and trees turned to gold
swans sang
and flew in symmetrical circles
fragrance filled the air
above your head
and sweet angels played
barry white
while you slept.

she said you wuzn't
suckled on her breast
but fed
nectar and ambrosia

the food due you as the only son
of zeus macbride.

i believed her.

cause you have always been
my religion
my daily invocation
my special sunday morning vespers
&
i am diggin'
the warmth n
style
of your
doo wop in a blue note
past
of your present redemption
yes
I'm feelin' it
right down in
the rectory of my lust

when preparing to lay with you
i don ceremonial beads
bloodthirst
gut
n the
red-tipped feathers
of the phoenix
sprout
from my singed curls
i take off my shoes
really
revealing my gnarly toes
you see
my kinks
my kitchen

(the nappiest part of my neck)   still

i sit before you serenely
whilst
the tannis root of love
bubbles and boils in my belly
its steam rising in my throat
filling the cave of my mouth
fat feast
spilling out peacefully
into the air between us

we bathe
in a love song which is
finally floral
our robes are covered
with the scent of
gardenias and sage
of freesia frankincense
n
freshly raked leaves
i reveal to you the source of
my ancestral tree

its trunk rooted in hell
me
the one remaining
barren branch
straining heavenward
toward peace of mind
you
suck away the
pain
welling up inside of me
the spider's bite poison
of narcissism
of vanity

24

(and it is rumored that
hattie macdaniels
may also have been seen
without that rag tied around. . . .
her head)

in that special place
just when i fear
the possibility of you
might make me
speechless
i find myself
whispering a serenity prayer
in your left ear
repeatedly

now
ain't that
religion?

CANIS RUFUS
(ode to chaka khan)

electric lady
knifin' the curtain
open with bejeweled fingers

> her head
> laden with citrus sweetened hairs—
> medusian ropes swingin' hot embers
> hennaed bells—
> her lips
> plentiful soft
> and smackin
> sweet badass's
> **TELL ME SOMETHIN' GOOD**
> her stomach
> stripped of all
> but bronze blue flesh—
> beaded rings of baby peacock feathers—
> her butt
> swayin' chains
> of lilies laced with sense-amelia—
> **MARRY DOOJAH WANNA FUNK WID ME?**
> her crotch
> explodin' light—
> mound of venus rainin' salt n flame
> on
> open   lifted   stadium   faces

she bodacious
she be

> jungle bunny   bessie smith   demoness
> howlin' at the moon

she be

> the voodoo chile jimi hendrix plucked
> strings to conjure up

she be

> the brass ring my mama said

good colored girls must not reach for
she be
        the circe
        that esoteric nut deigned
        to tell me was too much

she too literal
she too extreme
much too seamy
much too obscene
I say

SCREAM SISTA
your ward 8
sensibility
speaks for me
praise the day
I first heard
your illicit moans
ring stereo
in smoke filled
blue lit
basements

when my daddy said
SHE can't be music
give charlie mingus some play
make room for charlie mingus
ring in the new year wid . . .
nat king cole?

say?
can't be music?
if she
rushes in deep
my well
like poetry

like flush
like semen
like spit
like your bloodied face
reboundin'
one mo time
off the blows
of a so-called
black faced bimbo
broke down
from wailin'

                  nu blues

broke down
from wailin'

                  nu news

broke down
from
wailin' out
beyond image
to me
can't be music?

SONG OF THE SIREN

POEM FOR CARLEEN ANDERSON

language
flows fluid
through the wren
who sings freely

melancholic
bloodlines shade
her melody
hear how
sweet her
siren

on a nickelodeon stage
stealing kisses from
unsuspecting ears
insights break
the sound barrier like
cold chimes
ringing warning
through London's night sky

Circe's melody
how sweet she sings
lingua flows fluid through her

songstress linked to
Nile queens who have
reasoned well with infidels

her wisdom is like
NuNile stroked lovingly
through Cleopatra's
locks

every whisper
tells of
each suffering felt

Circe's melody
how sweet she sings
lingua flows fluid through her

BASQUIAT I & LAST

When you heard

You were a citizen
in this parking lot
county fair

You thought it wuz
time to Greyhound
outta here
& come back a drifter

Put it all in one bag

Left word in Sanskrit
& Scripture
it wuz not your intention

to linger
but

to resist
the white washing
Rinso actions
of moviestar footprints
n commodities exchanged
on the blood
& broken backs of
Kingfish & Sapphire

not
to haul in
sugar
tobacco
cane
copper

tin
the bauxite mines of Mandeville

not
        to procreate
salt

of
the
earth

AT A QUARTER TO FIVE

I still remember Cooley's Pub
the night
you sang a lullaby to me
as I passed out
    slowly
singin STAY
so sweetly
LIKE A LIDDLE BABY WHEN HE CRIES . . .
I gave you a case quarter for da replay
cause I thought you wuz
the
        real
             thang

gin stained sawdust
n
the sweet stench of
McSorley's Ale
draped
      loosely
round the pool lamp

me
leanin against the toilet door
damp and sticky
so you could

boot up
neatly
         the needle
your crisp
  starched
  shirtsleeves
without bloodstains

(it wuz beyond me)
tryin backwards to
bob and weave
hard earned dreams
into
temporal reality
you fled demons

I can hear you now
talkin about
the teachings of
H Rap Brown
or
RELEVANCE
or
"You me n the wild thing, my dear"

until

you slipped back
behind the blue shade

of Newport smoke n
        Billie Holiday
on your greying horse
        noddin
            noddin
                wid a soft sigh
unless

your nimble fingers
happened to
catch up the cue stick
in time
"da
8 ball goes in clean
we callin

all shots
banks n kisses
dat means
no near misses
my man!"

until

the lights went out
in mid-stroke
temporarily
that time
n
I know you meant well
"jus don't pay me no never mind
little girl. i'm goin to Carolina
in my mind . . ."
but you couldn't
stay
the inevitable

Each day
at a quarter to five
last stool
left corner
r&b n soda
twist of lime
twisted time
time twisted
twisted
the inevitable
turn of the cards
and
yours
wuz
up

QUEENIE

Queenie's screaming
from the black hole
she useta turn tricks outta
ain't nothin new
ha lips wuz always movin
makin necessary diva patter
—you know the deal—
deep head space literate
polysyllabic 10 dollar flavors
peppered with multiculti references
phrases strategically dropped in
conversations to imply a rich
varied
well-rounded tutelage

a most excellent sleight of hand

the suspect deck
stacked
paradoxically
in her favor

men loved the touch of her
cinnamon rosebud
fingers
her butterscotch
smooth palms
each glossy nail bed
recessed neatly
frenchly manicured

they loved her circular motions

"family secrets" she'd smile sweetly
"passed on by a distant

relation. ancestral. west indian."
they paid dearly for her mango treatments
for her scented breath hissing
softly at each stroke
"split the papaya, boy"
"eat the guava jelly"

those days
she haikued the expected
not she
the slackjawed smacking of gum
the spread-kneed meaty rump of a
healthy country drug dealer's girlfriend
splayed on a subway streetcar goin nowhere fast

Queenie required lavish
culture as well as
cash money
dom perignon, pouilly fuisse
the four seasons, the four tops
four aisles from the front
forty acres and

a black
four leaf
clover
etched painlessly on her left ankle
wuz
                how she
                                liked to
                                                think
                                                                it started
the predilection for . . .
her love of . . .
the needle
of the marks
of the drawing

of blood
of the black intricate
stories spreading
spider-like from
her crooked arm
of her burgundy-kohled
eyelids heavy wid stars
betraying a certain
marabou feather
tease
her hooker's caress
snaking the stranger's
thigh
bobbin'
bobbin' for quarters
butt up in the sun
bobbin'
bobbin' for a five spot
bobbin'
bobbin' to cop
dreams. . . .

it's 6:00
the 4th of July
Queenie's in deep space
behind a dead tree
she leans into
away from the rain
of firecrackers
rat-ta-tat-tat-tat
she leaps back
ragdoll
shaking her jagged hips

her hair
—radioactive strands of microorganisms—
is baying in the breeze

her
almond eyes
are
streaming
red slits

her ruby lips
are slack with drool

her daughter
waits
patiently park bench
watching mommie sideways
out one dry eye
steadily shredding
books while
Queenie screams
a silent aria
into the night sky

PRODIGAL: Dedicated To Mother Hale

she was annabella's daughter
yes lord
she was annie's child
brown and bacon thin
in need of a hot plate of greens

they brought her round to the house that sunday
said
miz emma
we puttin this lost lamb
in your hands to do the
lord's biddin
knew i
wouldn't be refusin
the work of the cross

not her
not nair one
of the thirteen other's
i took in
for gawd's will

her mama wuz one of my own
gone astray
berneatha was the
prodigal's orphan
come home

come a time
berneatha was
so grown
wasn't proper to
butter her legs on sunday
like the other chirrun

15 year old
and wild
couldn't hardly pass a hot comb
through that
hard head

skittish n short tempered
hardly ever home

had
two more
comin up behin huh
n my are-the-ritus
wouldn't 'low me
to be takin no more mess

berneatha said
ron l. wuz a
good working
kinda colored man
gentle n true

took sixteen hours to
ready the weddin dress
on the old singer
push n pedal
lord knows
the chile wasn't no bigger
than the space between ma teeth

took it in
twice the span
of two hands
laid together
side by side

made the

feast o jesus that day
butter babyback ribs
in barbecue sauce
hamhocks
macaroni & cheese
n aunt bessie's
black eyed peas
like for the
comin of a new year

right reverend i.e. winslow
presided over the ceremony
but berneatha would not eat . . .

when she said
she wuz in a
family way
wid ron l.'s seed
couldn't hardly see the child wuz acomin
she carried so
sickly n small

wouldn't let me tend to her
birthin in fever
screamin
ma em, ma em
don let em take my baby
don let em take my chile
& i say
hush sweetness
hush
they ain't worrin bout you
hush

first time i noticed them spots on her hands
didn't know what they wuz
n ron l.

walked out the door
in silence
it wuz the last i seen him

nobody said
not nobody said
not one doctor
not one nurse
nobody
not even the good lord
in his infinite mercy
had the
nerve
to tell a
christian
that this child's family
had been visited by the plague

or why
after 9 full moons
that firstborn
the beautiful baby boy
berneatha could not feed
would be
weaned
off bottle and
tube

yassur
they brought ron l. jr round to the house that sunday
said
miz emma
we puttin this lost lamb
in your hands to do the
lord's biddin
knew i

wouldn't be refusin
the work of the cross

not him
not nair one
of the fourteen others
i took in
for gawd's will

ain't studdin bout
why this chile has
aids
his mama
wuz one of my own
died today
the prodigal's orphan
come home

ASSISTANCE

I can type! Would you like to see me type?!

Camille sits at
her Executive Assistant's desk
son in lap
cramming moments
of normalcy
into corporate
maternity

she cannot feed
paper to platen
                    Where's RETURN?
I watch

silently

as she tries on
my life
blind
to that insult's
conceit

I covet
            the matching Pied Noire
nanny

vacations   in East Hampton

maids
            bringing coffee from the kitchen

her
Executive Assistant
older shrewder

hills of Virginia
considers it a privilege
to eat leavings
from boardroom meetings
she serves and
removes
with cutting eye
with narrow
high-chinned
condescension
she tolerates
Camille
sitting unapologetically
in the only seat
a secretary
can claim
her own

Camille Fairbanks
blue bred
salutatorian
class of '69
once sat cross-legged
by the campfire
loved intellect
married the intellectual
believed in freedom
the right to choose
carefully acknowledges
those who "do not matter"

she
never learned to type
never lifts headsets
never changes diapers
rarely sits with her son as he sleeps

I watch her loping figure recede
I watch
glued to my chairs
      my typewriters
          my landlords
               my responsibilities
wistfully reminded
of a half-remembered dream
of autonomy
of flight

FOOD

two all beef patties
special sauce
lettuce
cheese pickles
onions on a sesame seed bun
mickey d's is Central
to 42nd & 2nd lunch-breaking
   on the fast track
i'm packin'
my mini backpack wid 2 big mac's
there's no time today
i'm late
but in my heart
if i had my way
i'd take a rhythm & grind
break

truth be told
my ultimate goal
is to feed
my thoughts
   & **soul**
with food i never make

i crave food
lovingly prepared
by the wrinkled supper-stained
hands of my grands
with creases in places
i remember them to be
their pots blackened by the oils of

            4000 seasons of history

auntie ancient's jambalaya recipe

with shrimp & oysters
or cooked onion rings
wid slivers of liver
fat back 'n beans

black-eyed peas collard greens
chaw chaw gullah rice
cocktails in cracked ice
dixie cups
juice
outta strawberry jam jars
sips & soft songs
ham hocks
draped on pork bones

sustenance
food

a 4000 season history

of nigerian roadside
mama puts
selling steaming
white yams with red stew
yassa chicken
maffa au legume
equsi soup with fou-fou

4000 seasons of history

of making ground
yield delicacies
abundantly
cracking the casaba melon
gently
picking the guava fruit
spiritually. . . .

five after 8
i'm working late
another day
i've passed the test

of streets stewing traffic
people scrambling faster
cars hiccuping
garbage trucks
belch

another day
another dollar
in every way
i vie for power
& indigestion's
the price i pay to win

but when i take a break
brown baggin it
in a public place
i dream of food
which makes me feel
whole again

GAUZE

munich 1985
on line for
orwell's 1984
my white
        slip
            dress
transparent
gauze

i stand in sunlight

i am 18

i hear
his uptempo
smile beam
through me
his amble
all elegant linen
rumpled temples
greying sweat

"hey baby" in
very
high
german

i'm thinking
"I cannot comprehend
the distinction
between the meek n
myles davis, so why try"

we walk
cobbled strasse

along the isar
chinese gardens
ramble
beech trees
mark
sunspot shadows
on our path
i see his ring.

i am old enuf
to know adultery
means mastery
so i hook him
a quick grin
sideways

beer

the dark garden
dense with
bilious faces
roly-poly maidens
in lederhosen n
bustiers
pick through
mazes of
steins n
potato skins

i cannot find one
trace of myself
in the area

kellerstrasse

it's safe to go home
but

i platter myself
before him

                            wholly innocence

one day
my
beaded crystal dress
n silver satin pumps
wid
lemon drop heels
will support an illusion

i am well dressed
therefore
i am lucid

on this day
my chaste
transparent
gauze
dress
slips willingly
into an
untenable
abyss
knowing nothing
of consequence

METAMORPHOSIS

her
colt 45
flip top
she dropped
gingerly
into an
overflowing bin
collapsing
on the corner
of ludlow
and houston
her reeboks
squeak cleanly
past
suspect lumps
of brown
biscuits & gravy
walking home
she's convinced
that
even in the bowels of the bowery
change can begin
with the ritualistic shedding
the molting
of old skin
as hard as
crisped fatback
left two days off the fire
by peeling away
secretarial sneakers
freshwater pearls
lace trimmed slips
and bifocals
weekends only
she became the kind of

loosehipped woman
who always saw fit
to ignore other folks'
comparisons of her
with the more unruly
parts of themselves
their truth
was too obvious
to be taken seriously
that she was a dreamer
a sleepwalker
who always smelled of money
even when she had none
who only ever lived
in the shadows of midnight's bright lights
and who never let on
that under the clear hiss of a hot shower
she was often left
alone to unfurl her flower
she began her nightly ablutions
by smoothing her brows
with dabs of sweet honey and lemon
and soaked her hammered toes
straight
in clear lavender water
body oiled
skin glistening
like mute stained silk
she slipped
daintily
into the larger image
stiletto heels
whalebone corest
crotchless seamed stockings
and
the
slim

black
suit

this metamorphosis
was as familiar to her
as the opening of old wounds
the transition brought with it
images
visions
her younger face
smilin and glintin sweat
like off the mississippi
glittering in a
sweet louisiana sunset
she'd look down
and her
de rigueur black suit
had sprouted patches of calico
bits of blue lace
ivory velvet
pumpkin seeds
her flat feet
were arched
bare
and blanketed by the red georgia clay
she kicked into dust
dancin in one place
she was laughin so hard
her hot breath
pushed the entire state of south carolina
straight into a six month long summer
but she couldn't get to where
she could taste the cane
sent special from florida
or even spit the seeds from her
grandfather's melons

tonight
round midnight
she would find herself an adequate partner
who would treat her like a lady
but still know how it's done
a buppie
like that one
in sharkskin boots and bowtie
screaming numbers
sobbing in mock rage
levitating her skirt
with disinterested eye
laying her open
on a desktop computer
or that barstool
or a technicality
and having his way with her
e-e-a-s-y
like brushin his teeth
she wanted one who was
lightning fast
and secure enough
to feed in God's
fanciest styes
with pigs
but without
ever soiling his suit
a real
mephistophelian treed
man
who might also
open the door
of his ferrari
right there
on the brooklyn bridge
and let his

flavor of the month
decant permanently
if he had a mind to

or maybe the
glistening insanity
of a freewheeling
former speedballer
like that one there
with the glint of the
undertaker in his eye
whose steady stare
sucked the life out of her
ten seconds before
his palm
made acquaintance
with her face
repeatedly
like a flat stone
skipping the surface
of a smooth
still
lake

most often
he
was one she kept in memory
in stasis
serene
and palatable
though he never let himself
be taken
only deeply felt
as the elusive bestower
of a single
kiss

FANTASY LOVER #5

I

Your scent preceded you
by ten feet
I sensed it well
before you'd slipped
silent beside me
or even turned my barstool to behold
your red-rimmed eyes
"Jamison," it whispered,
"with a twist of Drakkar Noire
or Pouilly Fume with
early dinner.
Neither one before five"
I heard the click of
the collarlatch on
my neckchain
It was clear your
hands were accustomed
to the leash
You were much too
comfortable in your
role my dear
You did not flinch
when
for a moment
I bared my teeth
I noted your nails
were very finely
manicured
buffed to a subtlety
numbing sheen
You have ten thin
delicate fingers
two 18-karat gold cufflinks
and one micro thin Rolliflex

Which I let
brush my cheek
briefly
As your whiskey-dipped
pinkie passed leisurely
over my lips
for several seconds
then you asked me
for my name
I, of course,
would not give it
so our dance could begin
Again
Again
Again.

II
Drip over me
(I want rivers)
kneel low and deep
creep
nice and slow
by my bedside
to see the storybook
'neath my sheets.
I'll hiss Arabian
flavored fairy tales
about Sheherazade
unleashed
of her ruby red lips
sucking
gunmetal
feathers
binding
her lover's feet.

And when my rhymes are done . . .

Look at me
long and steady
let me sink my teeth
into your virgin flesh
and rip the logic
from your
protestations.

Let me
skate 'round the
crust on your heart
dismantling it bit by bit
and I promise
I will sip the
cool restless
sense of summer
from your
moist lips
and together
we'll drip
rivers.

III
YOUR
dreams
are of lusty ladies
kneed
into position.

Warm butterscotch bottoms
rise invitingly to meet you.

Their eyes,

poised between consent and contempt,
loll lazily

                    out of
reddened slits
                        into
K-Y jellied palms.

Nine inch
cherries in the snownails
dig
in.

YES-S-S

bellies   splayed
arms   forward
senses   akimbo

banana-soled feet
turned upward to meet
your   slapping groin
your   serpentine tongue
        eliciting sweet
        hot-breasted
        s-i-i-i-i-i-i-g-h-s. . . . l.

Issued on cue.

or
as you most prefer
in block-long queues.
(I stand somewhere off center
eyeing the newspaper)

I asked you for black leather
you're
givin' me
white lace!!

AVENUE B ARABESQUE

he has nothing
to bring to the table
no cards
no money
just

a hiss of thigh
whispering around her waist
brushing against her lampshade

his nicotine stained fingers flicking ashes
on her newly scrubbed
black and white tiled floors
making her skip one beat too many

his loose front tooth cap
causing a stench
he doesn't bother picking up

they make
havoc all over
his
dirty laundry
heaving & sweating
amid the
shards of glass
bottlecaps
bobby pins n
bits of paper
outlining his
pissed stained
mattress on the floor
beside a gate-crashing
black g-string
—absentmindedly forgotten by

a contender from
the night before—

a belligerently
gruesome duo
arabesquing near
a nicked up
baseball bat
leering
by the door
he slips his tongue
along her delicate underthigh
before slamming her
face against a wall
lipstained in shades
which do not suit her
but include those
she's worn before.

they rollercoaster
from despondency
to despair
the hallucinatory silence
broken only by his
rhythmic breathing
falling faster
the faint rasp of his
perpetually blocked
sinuses ensuring
hours of conversation
will again be entombed
in her head
which says

all she really wants
is a Sunday morning
subway ride

to Coney Island
& a Nedicks hotdog
hold the relish
until the Cyclone's
first
      free
            fall

HARD BARGAIN

i'm a bargain hunter
so
naturally
i thought i was
getting a
relationship rebate
when you
confided you
were easy
work

a former
bouncer in a *"titty bar"*
now unemployed
but light
years away
from the day you
took apart *"some girl"*
limb by limb
in the back of a
pickup truck
when you were

just fifteen
doing time in
juvenile detention
until the system
conveniently forgot
your crime
putting you back
on the streets of L.A.
deeming you
a hopeless case gone good
& clean
& sober

your speech pathologist mother
getting into the game
placing you in a special needs program
finagling a guidance counselor
finding you the college of
her dreams
she thought you would teach

you did
act like you had some sense
sounding s-o-o-o good
on my answering machine
your honey voice promising
the odd pat
n tickle
responding to every question
with yes & a smile
on the bad side
of Brando desire

strange
i thought i
might mend you
like a Rose is Vintage sweater
sewing dropped stitches
adding grosgrain ribbon trim
affecting a '50's
chanteuse persona wash n wearing
you to the bone

cool
noone need
ever know you'd
been bleeding
ulcered secrets
i was sure

you would tell me
in time
we would happen
right
     then
          i found myself
standing
in your kitchen
a modern day
aunt jemima
liberated from yr
roach infested
pancake box
serving up griddle cakes
grin plastered all over
my face completely
incredulous 'cause
i can't cook

then
waking out of an
emotional blackout
at a corner
phone booth
on 2nd & B
screaming like a
banshee on speed
destroyed
'cause you
hadn't invited me to
barbecue in Brooklyn
with Phoebe & her friends
remembering

i can't stand Phoebe

clearly

i'd become an extra
in my own
made-for-television movie
& had given
you
the lead

which is how
i came to this
mama said
conclusion—

some breaks
don't need fixing
when the effort
makes one bleed

FANTASY IN B-FLAT

How did they feel?
the shoes
which fit the feet just so
        the fine leather

How did they look?
the nails
impeccably glossed
                the delicate hands
creamed   to soft radiance

when did the neck
(balancing the head so sublimely)
enhance the coil of hair
        which strayed from others
                arrayed seductively
                        across our pillow?
How deeply
did her nails dig your flesh?

Were they
as painful as mine
which bleed my palms
as I pull the trigger?

SAVE THE ROBOTS

6 am on a weekday
morning
I au • tom• a• ton
into the back of
a white
      stretch
           limo
with a man I
        just
         met

whereupon
turning from the fully stocked bar
to ask for a match
I notice

He's got his
      fully
         erect
            six inches
                   in one hand
              a
          loaded
       gun
     in the other
        I grab the gun

my mind flashcard's
a second opinion
which says

A quarter pound of beef will make a burger
juicy
not too lean
the same amount of meat

can be
stuffed into a sausage skin
the hue and shape of which
would not be unlike
this pop-up Johnson
slung
in my face
before daybreak
with no subtle humour
& no apology
I am not amused
and
—being vegan—
don't
EAT
meat

I am well aware
a curious reversal
has taken place
he who assumed
WOMAN
synonymous with
glittering ornamental vacuum
is stunned by my decisive action
which is not merely
a question of discipline
but
of fearlessness
                              born
of my having been
skinned without the benefit
of anesthesia
before

I back out of the car
his obscenities blast

the air behind me

"bitchdykewhore!"

his contradiction in terms,
made all the more
poignant by my run for safety

scrambling home
remembering other nights
of salty teeth &
curious poses
of transient men
serially discarded
I wonder
what words
if any could
accurately
describe me

TOO ME (HEAVY MELLOW)

If I wear bells on my toes
beat a ring through my nose
bang a tom-tom till crack of dawn
upsetting **PC** politicos
whose idea of the
proper black aesthetic
may not include allusions to
Stephin Fetchit

n

If I play my music LOUD
stomping up a jackhammer
funk-a-licious on a religious
observance day

If I
         hook a
spangled nose ring
to my nipple
         wrap a
clashing feathered boa
round my Kangol
         spray my
fresh Puma skips
green and purple
declaring my new aesthetic
heavy mellow

If I sit absentmindedly
shange-like
legs open in a skirt
'cause that's how I do
my best thinkin'

If my bed's a
stinking cesspool
of well-worn
day-old chicken
of backlash books
of bell hooks
& poems
   from the Nuyorican

If my hair is deadup
straight on one side
and tell-tale
nappy as the day is long
on t'other

If my ears unwittingly
fill with wax
the minute you
whisper you love no other

If I speak too obtusely
splattering my food as my
friends stare on wonderingly

If I inadvertently
decide
to be
deliberately
unladylike
provocatively
tangibly
free

It does not necessarily follow
though you
understandably

may not agree
that I am *less* of a Woman
when I'm enjoyin' *more*
of me

HOUSECLEANING

Tonight
I was a mystery woman
who wasn't pretending to be
because I was truly a mystery to myself

I sucked my teeth in rage
and saw they were
green
from too many
days of neglect
I kicked the door behind you
and found my heels
were
calloused and cracked
from
running
in pursuit
of you

I sat before
my splintering
wood panelled wall
bits of plaster
on the floor
fallen from the ceiling
which caved in
after the
few short weeks
I was alone
again

You always said it would

You always said my
surname was disaster

and that was why
you
split

I fear for my safety

More often
I fear my own self
reflected
thank god the only mirror I own
is caked with dirt
I haven't been home often enough
to tend to it
I was too busy
following
you

I watch
minute particles of dust
resettle on the blanket
I just shook
and yet

I long for you

I want you to take me in your arms
and embrace me
like a lover
of
really
fine
things

I want you to taste me with relish
succor me
until the wellspring of my
bottomless desires

has filled up
despite my loneliness
with myself

allow me to be myself
allow me to be separate enough
to love you
properly
unbind me from the weave
of your checkered past
release me lovingly
tell me your name
not Michael or Beau
Sequoia or Jim
or any of the others I've
fallen
in with
tell me YOUR name
give me permission
to
clean
my
house
release me lovingly
Daddy . . .

SOUL OF THE PEOPLE

the Soul of The People
lives

> in the doo-wop bebop of
> Newjack Attitude

> in Yardbird Louie's
> bootblack blues

> in porters humming hymns
> on Park Avenue

the Soul of The People
lingers

> in fast fingers
> at Hattie's Hair So New

> in the dreams of downtown
> peddlers who ain't been here long

> in subway hieroglyphics
> in handwriting on tenement walls

the Soul of the People
skips

> sideways wid dookie braided
> sisters into public schoolyards

> wid bread n butter
> black to the bone brown poets

> wid sunday drummers
> on a quiet lawn

the Soul of The People
lasts

> in the Sista Reverend's
> laying on of hands

                              in the Honorable Brother's
                              revolutionary plans

in the   congas
in the   dejembe
on the   stoop
in the   alleyways
in the   red
in the   black
in the   yellow
in the   green

NOMMO

the power of the word
to elude the young poet
at a moment's notice
especially

when your panties are down
when the press called in
demands
you explain
the cogency of flatted fifths
or
why that
rum butter recipe
made its way
into the fifth stanza

at such times
you
MAY
indeed sigh

> "'Language has left
> me bereft of
> all i aspired to be.
> Try me tomorrow,
> please"

but
if that silence
doesn't speak
your voice
what then?

If you don't banter
with candor
with
idiosyncratic phrasing

with
semantics all
ill thought out
yet lovingly conceived

do you really think
someone else will
wait your turn to
wave the white flag
or find time to revile
the republic for which it stands?
dare to live
in the poet's space
round the myth
where poets
don't fear
mortal sin but
are
brown rubber
& poetry shapes itself
organically
within you alien
sinew entwining
itself between yr
wastrel brain & clarity
making language
seem
incandescent
light yet
not destroying
yr intellect
'cause like brown rubber

poets adapt

you MAY skirt
the issue

fearful of the truth
of poetry which
comes to you in
subtle dreams
willfully
bringing
all its joy
all its tomorrow
when you MAY
answer in kind
with a poem . . .